Sammy Sea Otter

Cindy Shanks

AuthorHouse™
1663 Liberty Drive
Bloomington, IN 47403
www.authorhouse.com
Phone: 1 (800) 839-8640

© 2017 Cindy Shanks. All rights reserved.

No part of this book may be reproduced, stored in a retrieval system,
or transmitted by any means without the written permission of the author.

Published by AuthorHouse   06/13/2017

ISBN: 978-1-5246-9642-9 (sc)
ISBN: 978-1-5246-9643-6 (e)

Print information available on the last page.

Any people depicted in stock imagery provided by Thinkstock are models,
and such images are being used for illustrative purposes only.
Certain stock imagery © Thinkstock.

This book is printed on acid-free paper.

Because of the dynamic nature of the Internet, any web addresses or links contained in this book may have changed since publication and may no longer be valid. The views expressed in this work are solely those of the author and do not necessarily reflect the views of the publisher, and the publisher hereby disclaims any responsibility for them.

Hi! My name is Sammy, and I was born in Morro Bay, California. I love living in the ocean, but I had a lot to learn from my mom before I could swim out into the deep water by myself. Come and visit the bay with me, and I'll share my story with you.

My mom was pregnant for six months before I was born in the salty bay. When I was born, I was covered in thick, light brown fur for a few weeks. My eyes were blue, but they turned black when I got a little older. I drank my mom's milk about 12 times a day. Mostly, I slept.

My mom kept me very close to her, so I slept on her belly as we floated around. We stayed close to shore because that's where mom would dive for the foods she liked best. When mom was hungry, I had to float on top of the water all by myself. I cried and cried until mom returned with her food and let me climb back onto her belly.

I crawled all over mom to find the best place to sleep. When I would wake up, I liked to touch her face and her whiskers. Her fur was soft and her whiskers were really long. She used her sensitive whiskers and her paws to find food when she dove deep into the water.

As I got older, I would try a few bites of mom's food. I had all 32 of my teeth when I was born, but mom had to teach me how to eat real food. I liked the same foods she did. Some of our favorites were crabs, snails, and clams. Mom would break the shells and give me the meat inside.

Even as a baby, I knew that I needed to keep my head, my paws and my flippers dry so they would stay warm. I don't have blubber to keep me warm like other animals who live in the cold ocean. I have two layers of skin, and mom would blow air into the fur as she groomed me so I would stay warm.

My mom was busy grooming both of us every day. Grooming is the most important thing we do, because it keeps us warm. But, I really hated it when I couldn't sleep or play because she was cleaning me all over, and I had to lie still.

When I was 3 months old, my fur became dark brown like the rest of the otters. That was when mom decided it was time to teach me how to groom myself. We have the thickest, warmest and softest fur you can imagine. First, I had to learn how to roll in the water to wash my thick fur.

Then, I learned to blow air into the fur. This helps to dry it, and adds warm air between the layers of skin. This warm air keeps me warm in the cold water. Sometimes, my mom would shake the water off her fur and it would fly everywhere!

Besides having very thick fur, we also have very loose skin. We can clean all over our body, front and back. We even have pockets under our arms because of our baggy skin. We can keep our food in these pockets of skin when we dive. We can also keep our favorite rock hidden there for breaking shells.

I still liked laying on my mom's belly, but now I was getting too big. My mom had taught me to swim and dive when I was about one month old. Now that I was growing up, I needed to sleep and groom myself in the water beside mom. I still liked to lay with my head on her belly and she liked to hold me very tight.

As I was growing up, I found that there were lots of fun things about otters that are special. My front paws look like I'm wearing mittens. But they are very special paws because I have claws that can come out when I need them, and then go back inside my paws.

Another special part of me are my back legs, which have huge flippers. I have very long, webbed toes that are different from your toes. My big toes are on the opposite side of my flippers than your big toes are on your feet. My flippers can pedal up and down on the top of the water, if I am not in any hurry, or they can flap sideways if I am diving quickly to find food.

As I was growing up, I realized that I could swim on my back just as well as I could swim on my front. After lessons from my mom and some practice, I learned to roll completely over with my head and paws out of the water. Since my head, paws and flippers have no blubber, I try to keep them out of the water to stay warm.

I learned to swim very fast, and I can move my body in lots of different ways because of my loose fur. That means I can get to my prey faster than other animals that want to eat the same foods that I do.

There were lots of babies born about the same time as me. When we were in the water together, we would play and make a lot of noise. Our moms would get tired of the racket, grab us by the neck, and tow us away from each other. We were in big trouble for a little while, and had to stay close to our moms.

Finally, my mom started teaching me more about finding food for myself. We would dive and eat three times a day. We had to eat a lot of food every day because our body uses a lot of energy just to stay warm. We can even dive at night because we have very good night vision, and our eyes have a special layer to protect them in the salt water.

One of our favorite places to eat was in the kelp forest. The kelp plants have large leaves called blades, and they grow in the calm water. They don't have any roots, but they attach to rocks to stay in one place. They have lots of bulbs filled with air that keep them floating upwards, growing towards the sunlight.

My mom loves the kelp forest because snails and crabs live along the tall stems. We can eat them as we move down towards the food at the bottom of the bay. One of our favorite foods is the sea urchin, and their favorite food is the kelp. We help the kelp stay alive by eating lots of sea urchins. If there were too many sea urchins, they would eat all the kelp.

The kelp forest is very important to many animals in the ocean. It provides calm waters for raising babies. It provides many types of food, and is a safe place for many animals to live. Otters have always helped to keep the kelp forests alive and healthy.

There are a lot of other animals that my mom taught me to eat. She showed me how to gather crabs, snails, and other foods in the bay, and carry them back to the surface in her baggy pockets. She then laid all the food on her belly, got out her favorite rock, and banged on the shells until they broke. The meat inside was delicious!

The seagulls circled overhead, waiting for us to finish our meal. After mom rolled over in the water to wash away the leftovers, the birds and fish ate what was left. Then, it was grooming time again. After cleaning our fur, it was time for a nap. We sometimes rolled up in kelp before we fell asleep, feeling safe because the kelp kept us from drifting.

Sometimes, we went hunting for abalone, one of our favorite foods. The abalone has only one shell, but the animal inside holds on tight to the rocks. Mom carried her favorite rock with her under her arm. She took out her rock and used it to bang on the abalone shell until it fell. She picked it up and carried it to the top where we had a meal on her belly.

When I was about 8 months old, I stopped drinking my mom's milk, and ate only what we found in the ocean. I had a lot of other young otters to play with. We played hard and rough. We explored new parts of the bay. We wrestled and had battles, often biting each other. I was getting prepared to leave mom, and go exploring alone.

All the moms stay close together in a group called a raft. They have a new baby every year, so they stay close to each other for protection. They have their first baby at 3-4 years of age, and live to be 10-15 years old. Throughout their lives, they never stray very far from where they were born and raised.

When the males are about 9 months old, they leave their moms and go out into the bay, and sometimes even farther out into the ocean, to live on their own. They sometimes travel several miles in a day away from shore. They will not become a dad until they are about 5 years old.

I was finally ready to go out to the deep water and explore the world on my own. My mom had taught me everything I needed to know, so I left the safety of the bay and headed out into the waves and the excitement of the open ocean. What surprises awaited me!

My first adventure was meeting people. In the bay, there were lots of boats, both big and small. There were people on paddleboards, people in kayaks, people on surfboards, and people just looking at me and pointing. I just kept moving farther and farther out into deeper and deeper water.

My first experience at finding food I liked was hard. There were no kelp forests, and none of the animals that I had eaten with mom. But, I could dive to the bottom and find something new and good to eat, like octopus, squid, and other delicious treats.

Then one day it happened! I saw my first whale! That was scary because I thought he might want to have me for lunch. I knew that many whales only eat small krill and creatures that will fit through their baleen, but the size of that whale still made me nervous.

The humpback whale paid no attention to me. I was too small to be dangerous, and too big for him to eat. He would dive down very deep, and then come back to the top with his mouth open, quickly filling it with small fish and krill.

The humpback was surrounded by birds who hoped to get some of his leftovers. They would land on him, and grab anything that jumped out of his mouth. I was so glad that I was not a food that he was interested in eating. After watching for a short time, I moved on.

The next animal I saw was a sunfish. He's the biggest fish we know about. He's very mellow, just floating around and eating, and letting the birds clean up his leftovers. I really like that white fin on his top.

On another day, I floated into a group of dolphins who were having a great time playing in the waves, leaping into the air with such joy. I tried to follow them, but they ignored me, and moved so fast I couldn't keep up.

I saw so many other animals that I'd never seen before. Some were beautiful, or ugly, some were scary, or just curious. One of the ugliest was an elephant seal. He was so big and mean looking that he really scared me. I thought about staying out from shore for a longer time, but I was very hungry for an abalone and some crabs. So, I decided to head back to Morro Bay and spend some time there.

As I turned and began swimming towards the bay, I watched a group of pelicans flying through the sky. They look beautiful when they fly in a "V" formation. I am sure I will see more of them when I get into the bay.

When I reached the bay, I was so happy to be home. I decided I would stay here and live in the clear, calm waters. I swam past a group of sea lions on a dock. They are so big and noisy that I decided to move farther into the bay.

As I got closer to the boat docks, I could see crabs on the rocks, and more good things to eat in the water. I might have to share some of my favorite foods with the herons who are watching the water for lunch, too. But, I think there is plenty of food for all of us who share the bay, and make it our home.

Every day at the ocean can be a wonderful experience. The water changes colors depending on the weather. The otters are active in different ways depending on their age and the environment around them. It makes each day unique and exciting. I hope you enjoyed learning and experiencing the ocean through Sammy's eyes.

Thank you to Fred Tillman and Steve Taylor for their knowledge and patience while helping me edit all my stories, and loving them almost as much as I do. You are the reason my books are the best they can be.

CPSIA information can be obtained
at www.ICGtesting.com
Printed in the USA
LVOW05s1910200717
542012LV00008B/25/P